T0055702

PIANO TIME PIECES

Book 2

28 companion pieces to Piano Time 2

new edition

Pauline Hall

MUSIC DEPARTMENT

OXFORD
UNIVERSITY PRESS

OXFORD
UNIVERSITY PRESS

Great Clarendon Street, Oxford OX2 6DP, England
198 Madison Avenue, New York, NY10016, USA

Oxford is a registered trade mark of Oxford University Press
in the UK and in certain other countries

© Oxford University Press 1989, 2004

The moral rights of the author have been asserted

Database right Oxford University Press (maker)

First published 1989
New edition 2004

All rights reserved. No part of this publication may be reproduced,
stored in a retrieval system, or transmitted, in any form or by any means,
without the prior permission in writing of Oxford University Press.
Enquiries concerning reproduction outside the scope of the above
should be sent to the Music Copyright Department,
Oxford University Press, at the address above

ISBN 978-0-19-372787-8

Music and text origination by
Barnes Music Engraving Ltd., East Sussex
Printed in Great Britain on acid-free paper by
Halstan Ltd., Amersham, Bucks., England.

Copyright acknowledgements

Gypsy tango (p. 16) by Gerald Martin © copyright control.

You can't keep a horse in a lighthouse (p. 27): words and music by Billy Clarges, Jack Hill, and Emile Littler. © 1937 B. Feldman & Co. Ltd, London WC2H 0QY. Reproduced by permisson of IMP Ltd, 161 Hammersmith Road, London, W6 8BS. All rights reserved.

Contents

Minuet	4
Breakfast time	5
Waltzing Matilda	6
Tarantella	7
The little hedgehog	8
Russian carol	9
My bonnie lies over the ocean	10
The wise elephant	11
Feeling fine	12
Allegretto grazioso	13
Gavotte	14
Auld lang syne	15
Gypsy tango	16
Rattlesnake rag	18
Climbing high	19
I hear a guitar	20
Five little frogs	21
Quadrille	22
Gigue	23
Russian winter	24
Swing low, sweet chariot	25
Grandmother's footsteps	26
You can't keep a horse in a lighthouse	27
The princess and the spinning-wheel	28
Holiday mood	29
Alabama bound	30
Valse triste	31
Rollercoaster ride	32

Minuet

Alexander Reinagle
(1756–1809)

Breakfast time

Alan Bullard

Waltzing Matilda

Australian song
arr. Pauline Hall

Tarantella

A Tarantella is a fast, whirling dance from Sicily. Dancing it was supposed to cure the bite of a tarantula spider.

Pauline Hall

The little hedgehog

Notice that your left hand plays in the treble clef. You only need to use fingers 1, 3, and 5 in both hands. When thumbs play, they are always on next-door notes. Listen for the prickles–on the first quaver of every bar–ouch!

There are only three chords in this piece:

Left hand: 

Right hand: 

Dmitri Kabalevsky
(1904–87)

Andante

mf

p

mf

Russian carol

This carol should sound very bright and crisp.

arr. Pauline Hall

Moderato

mf

p

mf

p

cresc.

f

My bonnie lies over the ocean

Scottish traditional
arr. Pauline Hall

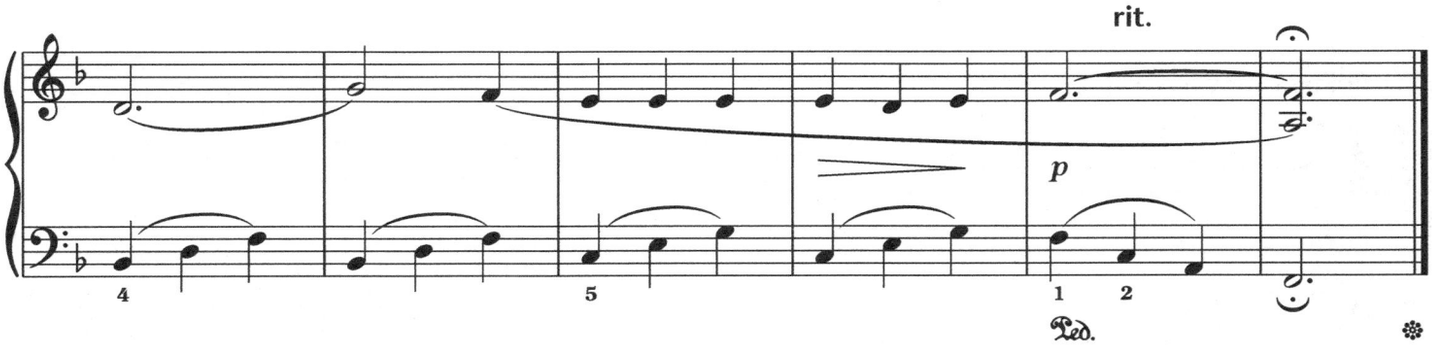

The wise elephant

David Blackwell

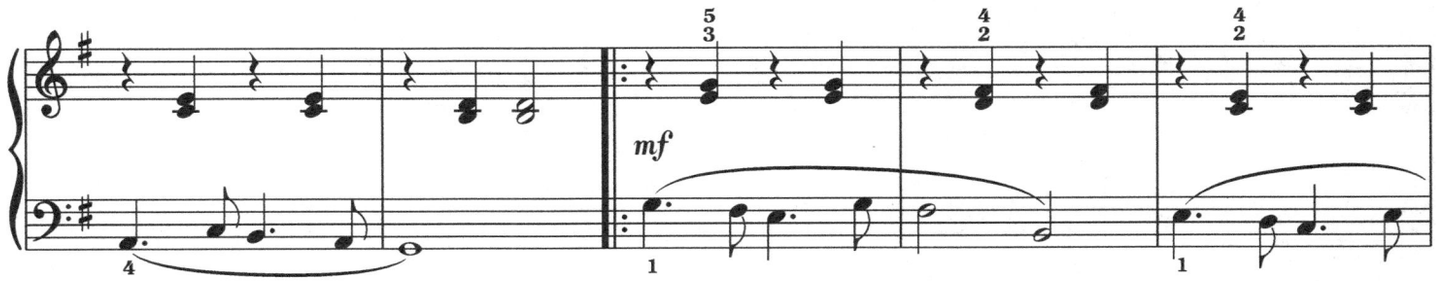

Feeling fine

Alan Bullard

Allegretto grazioso

Gavotte

James Hook
(1746–1827)

Auld lang syne

Scottish traditional

Gypsy tango

Gerald Martin

Moderately, with marked rhythm

f
mf
f

Rattlesnake rag

Steadily

Pauline Hall

Climbing high

Alan Bullard

Lively

p *mf*

f

p *mf*

f *ff*

I hear a guitar

Hansi Alt

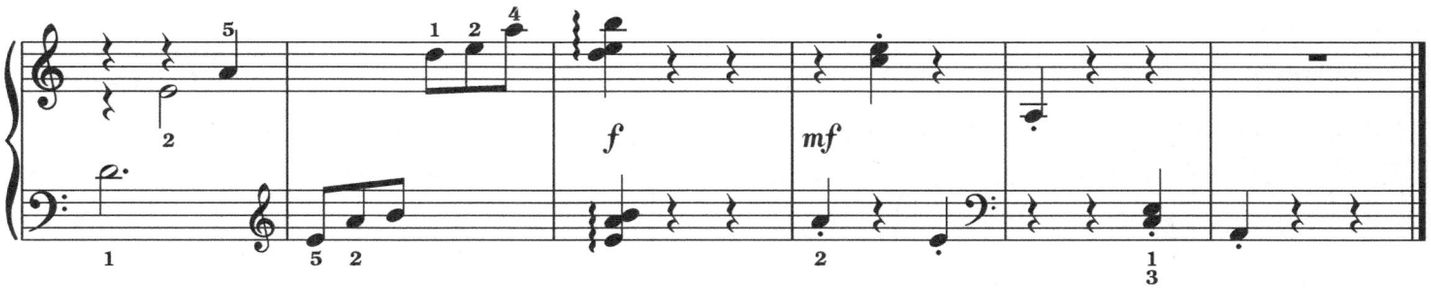

Five little frogs

L. B. Scott and Lucille Wood

Cheerfully

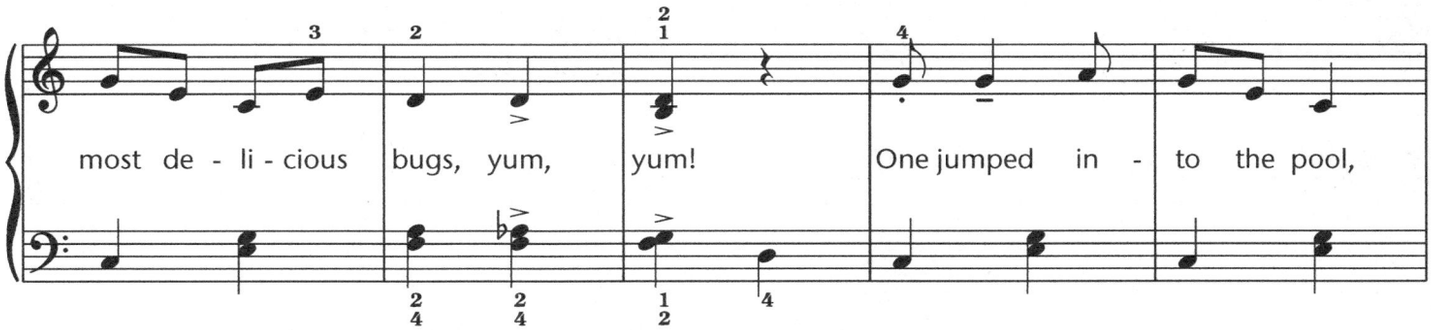

Quadrille

Alexander Reinagle
(1756–1809)

Gigue

Olive J. Wood

Lively

mf *mp* *mf*

cresc. *f*

mf

cresc. *f*

Russian winter

The sustaining pedal will help create the right atmosphere for this piece. Try pedalling once per bar.

David Blackwell

Swing low, sweet chariot

Spiritual
arr. Pauline Hall

Largo

mp

Swing low, sweet cha - ri - ot,___ com-ing for to car-ry me home.

Swing low, sweet cha - ri - ot,___ com-ing for to car-ry me home.

p *Fine*

mf

I looked ov-er Jor-dan, what did I see? com-ing for to car-ry me home. A

band of an - gels com-ing af-ter me,_ com-ing for to car-ry me home.

D.C. al Fine

Grandmother's footsteps

Paul Drayton

You can't keep a horse in a lighthouse

The princess and the spinning-wheel

As the princess sits spinning, she dreams about dancing a waltz at a grand ball. Make your playing tell the story.

Pauline Hall

Holiday mood

David Blackwell

Confidently

f

1.

2.

ff

Try playing the right hand part an octave higher on the repeat.

Alabama bound

American railroad ballad
arr. Pauline Hall

Valse triste

Rollercoaster ride

David Blackwell